All About
VIETNAM
Projects & Activities for Kids

Learn About Vietnamese Culture
with Stories, Songs, Crafts & Games

Tran Thi Minh Phuoc

Illustrated by
Nguyen Thi Hop & Nguyen Dong

TUTTLE Publishing

Tokyo | Rutland, Vermont | Singapore

Hello! Join us on an exciting journey to Việt Nam!

Contents

Hello, Friends! Chào Các Bạn!

Just like you, it's Hải Dương's first time in Việt Nam. With so many places to see, it's hard to decide what to do first. But who better to guide her than her two Vietnamese cousins. They'll teach us songs, tell us stories and introduce us to new foods, games and phrases. Best of all, they'll give us a close-up view of this bold and beautiful country. Let's go!

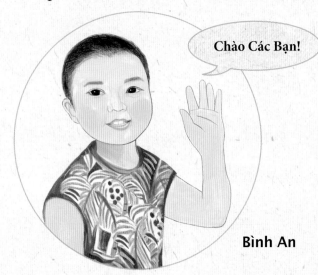

Chào Các Bạn!

My name is Bình An, which means "peace." My nickname is Ball because I have a very round face. I'm 12 years old and I love playing outside. I scramble across the monkey bridge and catch fish and shrimp with my bare hands. I also shoo the roosters back to the coop and ride sampans along the Mekong River. Both my parents were born in Sài Gòn. I'm the cháu đích tôn, or the firstborn grandson of the firstborn son.

Bình An

The Heavenly Lady Pagoda Chùa Thiên Mụ in Huế

Built in 1601 on Hà Khê hill, the eight-sided tower was rebuilt in the mid-1800s. According to legend, an old woman appeared one day on the hill and told the people that a kind lord would come and build a pagoda. She then disappeared without a trace. One day, Lord Nguyễn Hoàng came to the village and heard the story of the old woman. To honor her, he ordered a pagoda to be built. Today it's one of the most visited tourist attractions in Huế.

Chào Các Bạn!

Nguyệt Thu

My name is Nguyệt Thu, which means "autumn moon." I was born on the 15th day of the 8th month, also called Trung Thu, or the Harvest Festival, in Việt Nam. I'm 11 years old and live in Huế, the main city in central Việt Nam. My favorite foods are bún hến (a traditional Huế dish with noodles, herbs and tiny fresh clams), bún bò Huế (spicy beef soup with lemongrass) and bánh bèo (steamed rice cakes).

Hello my name is Hải Dương. That means "blue ocean." I was born in Minnesota in the United States. All of my brothers and sisters have the word "Dương" as part of their names. It means "blue." The color blue reminds our parents of how they floated for days in a crowded boat in search of freedom. I'm 10 years old and was born in the Year of the Dog. I'm the youngest of five children.

Cám ơn! Thanks for joining us!

Hải Dương

A farmer carries rice seedlings to be planted. Most of the nation's population lives in the countryside, where the people remain closely tied to the land.

Flower sellers head home for the day along the sand dunes of Mũi Né, a fishing and resort town on the country's southern coast.

People of the Mountains and the Sea

The Vietnamese people are known as the Children of the Dragon and the Fairy. According to legend, Kinh Dương Vương married a dragon's daughter. They had a son, Lạc Long Quân. The fairy Âu Cơ married the son and gave birth to a hundred eggs that hatched into a hundred boys. But the dragon loved the sea and the fairy loved the mountains, so they parted ways. Half went to live in the mountains with their mother and the other half lived with their father in the sea.

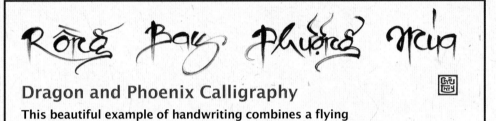

Dragon and Phoenix Calligraphy

This beautiful example of handwriting combines a flying dragon with a dancing phoenix. Can you copy it on paper?

The Vietnamese Dragon

has horns, scales, a snake's body, a buffalo's ears, fish eyes, eagle claws and tiger feet. Dragons can be found throughout Việt Nam on the roofs of palaces and temples, on carved furniture and bridges. In Vietnamese culture, the dragon—known as rồng or long—is one of the four mythical and sacred animals called Tứ Linh (see page 30).

A Vietnamese Proverb:
Rồng đến nhà tôm

"The dragon visits the shrimp's house"
This is used by a humble host to describe an honored guest.

Vietnamese farmers have learned to make the most of the sometimes rugged terrain. Their fields twist and turn following the curves of the land. These unique terraced rice fields look like green stairways or sculptures. They show how the Vietnamese have turned the land to their advantage.

Many places in Việt Nam bear the word "Long" (which means dragon). Sông Cửu Long (the Mekong or "River of Nine Dragons"), Hạ Long Bay, Long Hải Beach and the Hàm Rồng Mountain are some examples. Here, junks pass along the calm surface of Hạ Long Bay.

A Brief Look Back in Time

Let's take a quick look at a few highlights of the nation's past and some of the people who shaped its history. From rival kingdoms to the civil war, the Vietnamese people have faced many challenges throughout their colorful and dramatic history.

Sisters on a Mission

The Trưng Sisters, known as Hai Bà Trưng, (seen at left) are the nation's heroines. Trưng Trắc along with her sister, Trưng Nhị, and an army of 80,000 soldiers made up mostly of women, led the first revolt against the Hán invaders. The Chinese were driven out in 40 C.E. The sisters became queens, and established their capital at Mê Linh. Their reign lasted only three years though, as China regained control in 43. The Trưng sisters threw themselves in the Hát River rather than surrender. Today, many statues and shrines honor their heroism.

The Battle of Bạch Đằng Giang

in 939, ended a thousand years of Chinese rule. The general Ngô Quyền defeated the Hán Army by lining a riverbed with iron-tipped spikes. When the tide went out, the enemy boats were trapped on the sharp tips of the spikes.

Emperor Nguyễn Huệ

ruled from 1788 to 1792. Along with his two brothers, he led the Tây Sơn Rebellion. After learning that the enemy planned to attack at New Year, he ordered his soldiers to celebrate Tết earlier than usual. He then caught them off-guard. During his reign, new schools were established, and Vietnamese became the official language.

What Year Were You Born?

In Việt Nam, it's common to hear people ask, "What year were you born?" instead of "How old are you?" Each year is associated with one of twelve animals. In the West, children turn one year old twelve months after their birth. In Vietnamese culture, newborn babies are considered a year old at birth, because people view a pregnancy as a full year of life.

Mouse Tý

Resourceful, Thrifty, Quick-Tempered and Charming

1936, 1948, 1960, 1972, 1984, 1996, 2008, 2020, 2032

Buffalo Sửu

Determined, Dependable, Trusting and Patient

1937, 1949, 1961, 1973, 1985, 1997, 2009, 2021, 2033

Tiger Dần

Sensitive, Confident, Passionate, Daring and Brave

1938, 1950, 1962, 1974, 1986, 1998, 2010, 2022, 2034

Cat Mão

Affectionate, Skillful, Quick, Gentle and Cautious

1939, 1951, 1963, 1975, 1987, 1999, 2011, 2023, 2035

Dragon Thìn

Enthusiastic Intelligent, Confident and Strong

1940, 1952, 1964, 1976, 1988, 2000, 2012, 2024, 2036

Snake Tỵ

Creative, Attractive, Wise and Soft-Spoken

1941, 1953, 1965, 1977, 1989, 2001, 2013, 2025, 2037

Animals with a positive influence on each other bring fortune, success, and luck, also known as Tam Hạp. These pairings include:

Tiger- Horse- Dog; Pig-Cat-Goat; Monkey-Mouse-Dragon; Snake-Rooster-Water Buffalo

These incompatible years can have a negative influence on one another, known as Tứ Hành Xung. These include Dragon-Dog-Water Buffalo-Goat; Mouse- Horse- Cat- Rooster; Tiger-Monkey-Snake-Pig.

Horse Ngọ

Cheerful, Energetic, Funny, Active and Friendly

1930, 1942, 1954, 1966, 1978, 1990, 2002, 2014, 2026, 2038

Goat Mùi

Thoughtful, Gracious, Friendly, and Compassionate

1931, 1943, 1955, 1967, 1979, 1991, 2003, 2015, 2027, 2039

Monkey Thân

Ambitious, Adventurous, Smart and Quick-Witted

1932, 1944, 1956, 1968, 1980, 1992, 2004, 2016, 2028, 2040

Rooster Dậu

Intelligent, Brave, Stylish, Hardworking and Honest

1933, 1945, 1957, 1969, 1981, 1993, 2005, 2017, 2029, 2041

Dog Tuất

Trustworthy, Artistic, Loyal, Sincere and Friendly

1934, 1946, 1958, 1970, 1982, 1994, 2006, 2018, 2030, 2042

Pig Hợi

Studious, Modest, Easygoing, Joyful and Smart

1935, 1947, 1959, 1971, 1983, 1995, 2007, 2019, 2031, 2043

Let's Make a Dragon Puppet!

You can have a dragon parade with this long, slinky and colorful dragon! It's great fun!

YOU WILL NEED

1 piece of cardstock for the template
2 large popsicle sticks
1 piece of red cardstock for the body
Markers or crayons
Glue
Scissors
2 googly eyes (18 mm)

INSTRUCTIONS

1. Print out the dragon template on the cardstock. The link is: www.tuttlepublishing. com/all-about-vietnam
2. Color the head and tail in red or any bright, bold color you choose. Highlight the lines with dark markers. The claws should be black.
3. Cut the colored pieces to make the head, tail and feet.
4. Cut the red cardstock into two lengthwise strips 2½ inches (6⅓ cm) wide, glue them together to make a long strip before folding into accordion-style pleats (fold it, turn it over, fold it, repeating until done).
5. Glue the head, tail and feet to the body, then attach the popsicle sticks, one in front and the other at the back of the body.

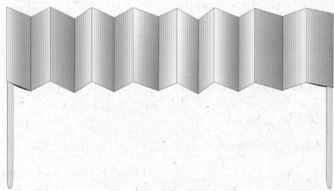

Your dragon is now ready
to join in the parade!

Learn a Little Vietnamese

The official Vietnamese language is called Tiếng Việt or Quốc Ngữ. It uses a writing system developed in the early 1600s by a Catholic missionary, Father Alexandre de Rhodes.

Some Common Vietnamese Phrases

How are you?	Ông or Bà mạnh không?	Ong, Bah mahn khon?
I'm fine	Tôi mạnh	Toy mahn
Thank you!	Cám ơn	Kam ung
You're welcome!	Không có chi!	Khon kah chee!
Excuse me	Xin lỗi (ông, bà, cô, em)	Sin loy
My name is . . .	Tôi tên là . . .	Toy ten lah . . .
What's your name?	(ông, bà, cô, em) tên gì?	(Ong, bah, ko, [e]m) ten zee?
Is that right?	Có phải không?	Kah fie khon?
Right	Phải	Fie

Two Syllables Become One

Westerners generally combine two Vietnamese words or syllables into a single word when writing local place names, such as Vietnam (Việt Nam), Saigon (Sài Gòn), Danang (Đà Nẵng) and Hanoi (Hà Nội).

Foreign Influences

Because the country was a French colony for many years, the Vietnamese language has many loan words from French. Some examples are: bom (*pomme*/apple), sơ mi (*chemise*/shirt), búp bê (*poupée*/doll), cà rốt (*carotte*/carrot) and pijama (*pyjama*/pajamas).

What's in a Vietnamese Name?

Vietnamese names are written with the family name or surname first, followed by the middle name and the given name or personal name last.

My full name is Trần Quốc Bình An
(Trần = last name, Quốc = middle name, Bình An = first name)

My full name is Lê Thị Nguyệt Thu
(Lê = last name, Thị = middle name, Nguyệt Thu = first name)

13

Hello, Hà Nội!

First, let's visit Hải Dương's paternal grandparents and parents' birthplace. Then, we'll cool off in Hạ Long Bay with its 1,600 beautiful islands and inlets. Finally, it's time for a tour and maybe a show!

Hạ Long Bay

Hạ Long Bay is a three-hour drive east from Hà Nội. It's our favorite spot. We love the beautiful blue water, the green islands, the tourist boats, the limestone mountains and of course the sunsets! Legend has it that long ago a family of dragons was sent to Earth by the Jade Emperor to protect the Vietnamese against northern invaders. During the battle, the mother dragon breathed fire while the baby dragons spat out jade and jewels, which turned into islands linked together by jade blue waters. The place where the mother dragon entered the bay is called Hạ Long Bay (Descending Dragon Bay) and Bái Tử Long Bay (Bowing to Baby Dragons Bay) is where the little ones swooped down from the sky.

The Temple of Literature

Also known as Văn Miếu Pagoda, it was built in 1070 by Emperor Lý Thánh Tông in honor of Confucius. The temple is divided into five courtyards and hosts the Imperial Academy (Quốc Tử Giám), Vietnam's first university. In the late 1400s, Emperor Lê Thánh Tông ordered stone tablets to be built on carved stone tortoises to honor the scholars who received degrees.

Water Puppet Shows

Water puppets are unique to northern Việt Nam, dating back over a century. The stories are drawn from Vietnamese folklore and include tales of fairies and national heroes. The plays are performed in a pond built next to a house or temple. The most beloved puppet is Chú Tễu (Tễu means "laughter"), a cheerful narrator who leads the show and draws lots of laughs from the audience. All the puppets are carved of wood. The puppeteers are behind a bamboo screen and control the puppets using bamboo rods and strings hidden under the water.

Vietnamese Folk Arts

The most popular folk arts are found in Đông Hồ Village, in Bắc Ninh Province. Đông Hồ prints portray happiness, harmony, prosperity, peace and wealth as well as heroes and heroines. Shown below are a set of Đông Hồ prints of Vinh Hoa (Honor and Glory) and Phú Quý (Wealth and Nobility).

Honor and Glory   Wealth and Nobility

Đông Hồ woodcut of chickens

One Pillar Pagoda

This square wooden pagoda in Hà Nội, known as Chùa Một Cột, was built by Emperor Lý Thái Tông in 1049 as a tribute to Buddha. The pagoda looks like a lotus blossom rising from a pond. Legend has it that the emperor met the Bodhisattva of Compassion (Phật Bà Quan Âm) in a dream, who gave him a happy baby boy sitting on a lotus flower.

Let's Explore Việt Nam's Old Imperial Heartland

Now it's time to visit Nguyệt Thu's grandparents and her parents' hometown. Amazing architecture awaits and the street foods of Huế are among the nation's best. Whether you like palaces and temples or beaches and food, there's plenty to do in the heart of the nation.

Thanh Hóa

Quảng Trị

Huế

Đà Nẵng

Nha Trang

Golden Dragon Bridge

This six-lane bridge over the Hán River is one of the most memorable crossings you'll make in Việt Nam. The slithering body of a dragon stretches gracefully across this river in Đà Nẵng. The bridge opened on March 29, 2013, and has been a main attraction ever since. At night, tourists and residents take in its 2500 lights. On weekends, the dragon comes to life, breathing jets of water and lighting up the sky with fire.

The Mausoleum of Emperor Khải Định

Blending Eastern and Western styles, this tomb is located in Châu Chữ Mountain outside Huế.

Hội An

Hội An is a vibrant city popular with tourists. There's a lot to see and do here. A trading port since the 1400s, many different people and cultures have passed through the city, leaving their mark. Old Chinese shops, houses and temples, canals, colorful French-era buildings and the famous Japanese Covered Bridge are just some of the examples.

Huế's Tasty Dishes

In the old days, the best Huế dishes were served to royal families. But now everyone can taste these treats at local restaurants and roadside stalls. Huế cuisine consists of many small dishes with lots of fresh herbs and spices. Let's sample some delicious Huế treats made by Nguyệt Thu's mom.

Spicy Beef Noodle Soup   Bún Bò Huế

This is a soup everyone should try in Huế. The broth is made of beef bones, ginger, lemongrass, fermented shrimp paste, sugar, beef and pork. A plate of fresh garnishes, such as thinly sliced banana flower, onions, Thai basil, bean sprouts, lime wedges, chili and coriander leaves (cilantro) are served on the side. Added to the soup, they're the perfect finishing touch!

Tapioca Shrimp Cakes
(Bánh Bột Lọc)

Rice Dumplings
(Bánh Ít Trần)

Flat Rice Dumplings
(Bánh Nậm)

Clam Rice (Cơm Hến)

Other favorite Huế treats include tapioca shrimp cakes, rice dumplings, flat rice dumplings, clam rice and Vietnamese crêpes. Save room for the best dessert in Huế: lotus seeds stuffed with longan in a sweet soup.

A street stall sells the colorful, sweet soups in Huế known as chè.

Vietnamese Crepes
(Bánh Khoái)

It's Time for Tết in Sài Gòn!

Sài Gòn is especially vibrant during New Year's celebration known as Tết. The region also teems with life the rest of the year, from the islands and waterways of the Mekong Delta to the seaside resorts and wide-open beaches dotting the coastline.

Tết, the New Year

Vietnamese New Year is the most important festival of the year. It starts on the first day of the first month of the lunar calendar and lasts for three days. A week before Tết, we go to visit our ancestors' graves to clean and decorate them with fresh offerings and flowers, and burn incense. We invite the spirits to return home for the New Year's celebration.

Sounds of the Bamboo Pole

A bamboo pole is stripped of most of its leaves except for young branches at the very top. Wind chimes and other objects are attached to the pole to attract good spirits and chase away evil ones.

The Kitchen God

Helping guard and protect the home, the Kitchen God is often shown wearing a hat and shoes, but no pants. In some versions, he's pictured riding on a carp. Several days before New Year's Eve, he goes to heaven to report on the household. Grandma sends him on his way with special foods and goodies.

Lucky Red Money Envelopes

On Tết eve, called giao thừa, Grandma invites our departed ancestors home and offers them foods. One of our favorite Tết rituals is called mừng tuổi. It's a special way of sending good wishes for the new year. We fold our arms across our chest and thank our parents and grandparents for everything they've done for us. Our grandparents then give us blessings and good advice—and lucky red envelopes with money called lì xì!

New Year's Rice Cakes
Bánh Tét

These sticky cakes make a special appearance every New Year. Made of soaked rice, mung beans and pork belly, the cake is shaped into a log, wrapped in a banana leaf and steamed.

New Year's Symbols

- **Apricot Flowers** hoa mai
- **Bamboo Pole** cây nêu
- **Firecrackers** pháo
- **Lucky Red Envelopes** lì xì
- **Tết Couplet** liễn Tết
- **Candied Fruit** mứt

Lucky red envelopes on an apricot tree

Five-fruit Tray
(mâm ngũ quả)

Mai Yellow Flower

The Unicorn Dance
Múa Lân

The three cousins are so happy to be celebrating Tết for the first time together. Hải Dương is eager to learn the traditional Tết celebrations in Sài Gòn and join us in being the first visitor in the New Year.

Sights, Sounds and Tastes of Tết

Việt Nam comes alive with activity during Tết. The crash of gongs, the pop of firecrackers and of course lots of games and good wishes are on display. Let's learn some Tết greetings, as well as some superstitions connected with the festival.

A festive spread of typical Tết dishes

The Gourd Crab Game Bầu Cua

A very popular and noisy game played at home or in the streets around Tết uses a board divided into six squares. The squares have pictures of a a gourd (Bầu), a crab (Cua), a fish (Cá), a deer (Nai), a rooster (Gà) and a shrimp (Tôm). Players place bets on the square of their choice. A banker shakes three dice in a dish covered with a bowl. If a player's chosen picture appears on the dice, he or she wins. If it's on one dice, the player wins the amount bet. Two dice mean twice the amount, while three dice yields three times the amount!

Learn Some Tết Greetings

- **Happy New Year** Cung Chúc Tân Xuân or Chúc Mừng Năm Mới
- **Peace, good health and prosperity** An Khang Thịnh Vượng
- **Wishing you good health** Sức Khỏe Dồi Dào
- **May all your wishes come true** Vạn Sự Như Ý
- **May money flow in like water** Tiền Vô Như Nước

New Year's Superstitions

- Wear red clothes and prepare red foods
- Be happy and wear a big smile
- Feed the unicorn red envelopes for good luck during the unicorn dance
- Don't sweep the floor at New Year, you'll whisk your luck away
- Don't whine or cry

Firecrackers and Gongs

The Vietnamese believe that making loud noises is a great way to greet the New Year. The pop of firecrackers and the ringing of gongs help to chase away evil spirits during the three days of Tết.

Peach blossoms
(Hoa đào)

Watermelon
(dưa hấu)

Sliced rice cakes
(bánh Tét)

Red lucky
envelopes (lì xì)

Candied fruit
(mứt)

21

The Bamboo Tree with 100 Knots

Bamboo shows up in many Vietnamese myths and legends. The brave warrior Saint Giong pulls up the tallest bamboo plant in the village to fight off invaders. During Tết, the bamboo tree drives evil spirits away and brings peace and good luck. Then there's the story of the Bamboo Tree with 100 Knots and its important lesson: One good turn deserves another.

Make Your Own Colorful Characters:

| The Young Servant, Khoai | The Master | The Master's Daughter | The Wealthy Man | The Old Man | The Bamboo with Knots |

Assign the six speaking roles. Don't forget about the Narrator!

Narrator: A young servant named Khoai worked hard for his wealthy master for many years for no money. He was only given food and a small corner to sleep at night. He woke up early each morning to feed the animals before heading to the rice fields. But the greedy master was never satisfied with Khoai's work. He treated all of his servants badly. One by one, they quit, leaving only Khoai. The Master became worried that Khoai would leave too.

Master: What can I do to convince Khoai to stay?

Narrator: The greedy master paced anxiously back and forth. Suddenly he stopped with a mischievous grin on his face. He called out to Khoai.

Khoai: What can I do for you, Master?

Master: (Pretending to be nice) Please sit down. I want you to work harder in the next three years and, if you do, I'll give you my daughter's hand in marriage.

Narrator: Khoai couldn't believe what he'd heard. He was grateful for the master's kindness. Until one day . . .

Master: Hey, Khoai, go find a bamboo with 100 knots and make chopsticks for the wedding. Don't come home until you have one with 100 knots!

Khoai: Of course! I'll go right away!

Narrator: Poor Khoai, he didn't know the Master had tricked him. While Khoai was searching for the bamboo, the Master got ready for his daughter's wedding to the son of a rich landlord in a nearby village.

Khoai: 52, 53, 54, 55, 56 knots. Not enough, even though it's the tallest bamboo in the forest. Where can I find one with 100 knots? I'm so tired, I can't keep searching. Somebody, please help me!

Narrator: Khoai was exhausted. Then, much to his surprise, he saw an old man walking toward him.

Old Man: What's the matter, young man?

Khoai: I need to find a bamboo with 100 knots to make chopsticks for my wedding. It's my future father-in-law's request. But I can't find one.

Old Man (laughing): It's easy! Go cut 100 bamboo knots and I'll show you the trick.

Narrator: Khoai thanked the Old Man and started to cut bamboo. Finally he brought 100 bamboo knots to the Old Man, who told Khoai to line them up.

Old Man: Khắc nhập, khắc nhập! Stick together, stick together! Remember these magic words.

Narrator: Khoai couldn't believe that all 100 knots stuck together in a row. It was the longest bamboo he'd ever seen.

Khoai: Thank you so much!

Narrator: The Old Man disappeared. Khoai suddenly realized the man was actually Buddha in disguise. He was so happy to have the bamboo with 100 knots. But the bamboo was so long, he couldn't carry it back home. Feeling hopeless, he started to cry.

Old Man: What's wrong now? Why are you crying again?

Khoai: The bamboo is so heavy and long, I can't haul it home.

Old Man: Remember these commands, Khắc xuất, khắc xuất! Unstick, unstick!

Narrator: Before his eyes, all 100 knots separated. Khoai tied them up and carried them home. As he approached the village, he could hear music, laughter and drumming. He could see guests going to the Master's house. The wedding was about to begin. Khoai realized he'd been tricked. He dropped the bamboo knots in the front yard.

Master: You're a fool! I said a bamboo with 100 knots, not 100 bamboo knots. Get out of my sight!

Wealthy Man: Yes, get out of here! Today is my son's wedding day!

Narrator: Both men laughed as hard as they could. But Khoai started to say the magic words.

Khoai: Khắc nhập, khắc nhập! Stick together, stick together!

Narrator: Instantly the bamboo joined together and formed a long bamboo with 100 knots. The Master, the Master's Daughter, the Wealthy Man and all the guests couldn't believe it. They crowded around, curious to touch the magic bamboo.

Wealthy Man: Help! Somebody help me!

Master: Khoai, please forgive me and set me free. Let me have another chance. I'll keep my promise. You can marry my daughter.

Khoai: Khắc xuất, khắc xuất! Unstick, unstick!

Narrator: Khoai said the magic words to free everyone. The Wealthy Man and his son left in a hurry. The wedding continued with Khoai and the Master's Daughter. They lived happily ever after.

Birthdays, Weddings and Other Special Events

Before the French arrived, the Vietnamese did not celebrate birthdays. Times have changed, but still, certain key events are honored. Parties, feasts and festivities bring families, friends and communities together to celebrate weddings, honor the passing of relatives and to mark milestones in a child's life.

A Baby's One-Month Celebration

One month after a child is born, friends and family gather to meet the baby for the first time. This event is called lễ đầy tháng. They offer prayers for its protection and wishes for a long and happy life. The one-month celebration includes an offering of special foods to the Holy Godmother—the protector of children—who teaches the baby to smile, sleep, yawn, kick and move its arms and legs. During the celebration, parents often put new clothes on the child. The baby also gets gifts: money, gold bracelets, necklaces with lucky charms. The photo on the left shows a double celebration to welcome twins!

It's Your Birthday!

Birthdays weren't always celebrated in Việt Nam. In the past, getting another year older was part of the New Year festival of Tết. Then the French introduced the idea of celebrating birthdays. Along with the practice came the birthday party! Cake, presents, hats, streamers are all given a Vietnamese twist.

Predicting a Child's Future

Lễ thôi nôi is the traditional Vietnamese first-birthday celebration. It means "giving up the cradle." It's a time to give thanks to the ancestors and the 12 God Mothers for protecting and blessing the child. The best part of the celebration is the grab ceremony. Parents place several items on a tray in front of the child. The first thing the child grabs predicts his or her future career or destiny.

Sixty Years—A Full Life Cycle

A 60th birthday is considered a major celebration. It marks the end of a full life cycle. The family celebrates and honors the person with a big party. Gifts are given, and a feast is served. Children and extended family members gather round to celebrate the honored elder.

Wedding Ceremonies

The groom's family presents a range of gifts to welcome the new bride and her family into the fold.

A boat carries a wedding party along the Mekong Delta.

Offerings at the Death Anniversary

The death anniversary, called đám giỗ, is an important event for many Vietnamese families. Usually the oldest son prepares the anniversary feast and leads the rituals. Today, some families still burn small objects like houses, boats, fancy clothing or cars for their ancestors on their death anniversary. That way, their relatives can enjoy a comfortable and happy life after death.

Special Birthds

- 60th birthday Lễ Hạ Thọ
- 70th birthday Lễ Trung Thọ
- 80th, 90th, 100th Lễ Thượng Thọ

Elders are shown great respect. In any situation, honor and preference are given to the eldest member of the family or group. You don't eat until the oldest person at the table begins eating.

Who's Hungry?

"Ăn cơm chưa?" Have you eaten rice yet? is considered a warm and friendly greeting in Vietnamese culture. No gathering or family reunion is complete without a big meal or special food of some kind. Rice is eaten with many Vietnamese meals but noodles and bread are popular too. Small amounts of meat and lots of herbs and vegetables are typically added.

Above from Left to Right:
Beef Phở, Bánh Mì and Chả Giò

Popular Vietnamese Treats

Phở beef or chicken noodle soup, is a popular treat. For fans of sandwiches, Bánh Mì is crusty bread stuffed with pâté, cold cuts or grilled meat, fresh cilantro (coriander leaves), pickled daikon and carrots. Chả Giò, called Nem Rán in the North, are fried Spring Rolls stuffed with a range of fillings. They're a must-have snack or appetizer for anyone who loves Vietnamese food.

A popular treat, three-color dessert. Cold Vietnamese coffees and other drinks are often sold from food trucks.

A Typical Vietnamese Dinner

A typical family meal includes steamed rice, a soup, a meat or fish dish and a small bowl of fish sauce. Vietnamese people eat family style. The food is placed on the table and the dishes are shared. Children are reminded to finish the rice in their bowl as a way to honor the farmer and the food.

Street food: a cart sells Phở noodles

No matter what dish you're making, fresh ingredients are key. People go to the open markets daily to buy vegetables and common ingredients. Chicken, duck and fish are often added to the shopping list.

Phở with hoisin sauce (Tương)

Bean sprouts, basil & sawtooth herb

A vendor sells fresh vegetables door to door.

A street food stand with tasty Phở soup and Spring Rolls.

Let's Make Two Delicious Dishes!

Now it's time to try some Vietnamese dishes you can whip up in your own kitchen. With an adult to help you, you can make these tasty treats in no time. The sandwich has been adapted a bit (use whatever filling you prefer or have on hand). The spring rolls are good as appetizers, snacks or anytime. The peanut hoisin sauce is a modern, kid-friendly addition.

Bánh Mì Sandwiches

This lunchtime treat has become popular around the world with shops, food carts and food trucks putting their own spin on this classic combination. With the French bread, meat and fresh herbs and vegetables, it's a true fusion of French flavors and Vietnamese flavor.

4 SERVINGS

¾ lb (325 g) beef or 1 large boneless chicken breast
1 tablespoon olive oil
2 teaspoons minced shallots
1 teaspoon minced garlic
1 tablespoon honey
¼ teaspoon pepper
1 tablespoon soy sauce
1 tablespoon oyster sauce
1 teaspoon sesame oil
1 medium carrot, grated or julienned
1 medium cucumber, peeled, deseeded, cut into very thin strips
Cilantro (coriander leaves), to taste
4 French half-baguettes or similar long bakery-style rolls

1. Slice up the chicken and put it in a bowl. Marinate the chicken in the olive oil, shallots, garlic, honey, pepper, soy sauce, oyster sauce, sesame oil and put in the fridge. After 1 hour, sauté or grill the chicken.
2. While marinating the chicken, grate or julienne the carrot and prepare the cucumber.
3. Slice the baguettes.
4. Chop the cilantro. Assemble the sandwiches, adding more soy sauce, if desired.

Fresh Spring Rolls

Gỏi cuốn is a snack sold at food stalls across Vietnam. It takes a little practice to work with the rice paper wrappers. But once you get it, you'll be making fresh spring rolls like a pro! Use the fillings of your choice.

6 TO 8 SERVINGS

Twelve to sixteen 10-inch (25-cm)
  dried rice paper wrappers
32 mint leaves
16 large basil leaves
8 small lettuce leaves cut in half
¾ lb (325 g) medium-sized
  cooked shrimp

Peanut Hoisin Dipping Sauce
5 tablespoons hoisin sauce
2 tablespoons creamy peanut
  butter
½ teaspoon sugar
¼ teaspoon salt
1 tablespoon vinegar
Chopped roasted peanuts,
  for garnish

1. Have all your ingredients prepared and arranged in bowls near your workspace.
2. To soften dry rice paper, quickly dip the rice paper in a bowl of lukewarm water, no longer than a few seconds.
3. Place the softened rice paper on the wet board. Arrange lettuce, mint and basil leaves in a line about 1 inch (2.5 cm) away from the bottom edge of the wrapper. Line three pieces of shrimp about 1-½ inches (3 cm) above the vegetables.
4. Fold the bottom part of the rice paper wrapper over the vegetables. Continue rolling everything toward the shrimp. Once you reach the shrimp, stop and fold the left and right sides of the wrapper toward the center. Continue rolling until you reach the top and form a roll. Place the finished spring roll on a platter. Repeat for the remaining spring rolls.
5. Combine well the ingredients for the peanut dipping hoisin sauce and simmer on low medium for about 5 minutes so sauce can thicken. Adjust the seasonings to your taste and topped with chopped roasted peanuts. Transfer to a small bowl and place on the platter with the spring rolls.

Four Mythical Vietnamese Animals

These four sacred creatures represent the nation's strengths in animal form. These magical beasts can be found as sculptures and decorations in pagodas, temples, cemeteries and homes.

Dragon Long

With its chin beard, sharp horns, hawk's claws and fish scales, the Dragon also has a slinky, curving body like a snake. It's able to change the weather and the seasons, so it's an important creature to Vietnamese farmers.

Phoenix Phụng

With the neck of a snake, breast of a swallow, back of a tortoise, claws of an eagle, scales of a fish and tail of a peacock, the Phoenix stands for power and grace. According to Vietnamese beliefs, it only perches in very high places, preferably the Ngô Đồng tree, which is used for making musical instruments.

Unicorn Lân

With the body of an antelope, feet of a horse and a buffalo's tail, the Unicorn is a symbol of wisdom and kindness. It only appears on special occasions, sometimes with two horns instead of one.

Tortoise Quy

The Tortoise represents the world—the earth and the sky—as suggested by the shape of its shell. Tortoises also live a long time, so they're the perfect symbol of the nation's long life and long history.

Việt Nam's Native Wildlife

With its lush landscapes and many national parks, Việt Nam has a range of places for its amazing animals to call home: rivers and coastlines, tropical forests, damp caves and misty mountains. From the family dog to shy primates hiding high in the trees, let's meet four common Vietnamese creatures.

Great Hornbill

With a large "horn" on its bill, known as a casque, this bird really stands out. The beak is lighter than it looks though, filled with many hollow chambers. Hornbills love figs, eating up to 150 at a time. They're also a help to farmers, eating large numbers of insects and small animals that feed on crops.

Water Buffalo

As part of a Vietnamese saying goes, "water buffaloes pull the plow and are friends of the children." The unofficial national animal (there are about 3 million in Việt Nam), they're a key part of rural life. They help plow the rice paddies and haul carts of supplies. For many kids, it's their job to tend to the family buffaloes.

Red-Shanked Monkeys

These colorful monkeys get their Vietnamese name from the word for "torch": đuốc. They live in the treetops, in groups of about 4 to 15, in the jungles of central Việt Nam. Their coloring can range from ruddy brown to red-orange.

The Phú Quốc Ridgeback Dog

This rare dog breed is native to Phú Quốc, an island off the southern coast near Cambodia. It's one of only three breeds to have a ridge of fur along its spine that runs the opposite direction to the rest of its hair. This feature is found in many dogs in Vietnam, but there are only 700 purebred Phú Quốc Ridgeback dogs registered with the Vietnam Kennel Club.

Favorite Children's Games

It's common to see kids scoring goals on the country's many soccer fields. But Vietnamese children stay active and have fun in lots of different ways. From martial arts to board games to badminton, there's always something to do for Vietnamese kids on the go.

The Ball and Chopsticks Game Banh Đũa

This game requires at least two players, who take turns.

YOU WILL NEED
Any bouncing ball
10 chopsticks

How to Play

Step 1 Start by spreading all the chopsticks on the ground. Throw the ball up, quickly pick up one chopstick with one hand, while the ball is bouncing, then catch it with the same hand. The ball is allowed to bounce only once. Put the chopstick in your other hand before continuing to pick up the rest one by one.

Step 2 Spread all the chopsticks on the ground, then repeat Step 1 by picking up the chopsticks two at a time until you've gotten them all. Keep playing until you have four, six, eight, then all 10 chopsticks in your hand.

Step 3 Hold all 10 chopsticks together in one hand. Throw the ball up, while tapping the chopsticks on the ground 3 times. The ball is allowed to bounce only once. The player to complete all three steps wins the game. If the player drops the ball or can't pick up the chopsticks, his or her turn is over.

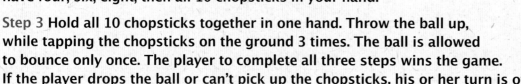

A Sack Race to the Finish

On your mark, get set, go! Kids in a bag? For a sack race, those are the rules. No one is sure how it made its way to Việt Nam. Was it something the French brought? Or did American soldiers first show local kids the race during the Việt Nam War? No matter what, it's a test of your hopping abilities to make it across the finish line.

Soccer Fans

Soccer (called bóng đá in Vietnamese) is the country's most popular sport. It's played in schools, public parks, on streets—everywhere and anytime a group of soccer lovers gets together. The French introduced the sport in the 19th century.

How to Count 1 to 10 in Vietnamese

1	một	mohk	6	sáu	sao
2	hai	hi	7	bảy	bye
3	ba	bah	8	tám	tahm
4	bốn	bone	9	chín	cheen
5	năm	nuhm	10	mười	meui

Vietnamese Hopscotch

Now let's play a game you might recognize. As you hop along, you can practice the numbers you've learned from the chart above. But pay attention, make sure you don't step outside the lines!

Yoga for Kids

Yoga has become hugely popular in Việt Nam today. Kids can take classes across the country. They love making the shapes of animals and trees while building strength and balance.

Let's Play the Dragon-Snake Game

Rồng Rắn Lên Mây, or the Dragon-Snake Game, is a popular pastime for Vietnamese children. Get a group of friends together and see if you can grab its tail.

Rules

At least 8 players including the dragon-snake and the doctor. Each player puts his or her hands on the waist of the person in front. Follow the dragon-snake's moves and try to make a circle before the doctor catches the tail. The game starts with the dragon-snake and the players singing on the way to doctor's house.

Doctor: Dragon-Snake, where are you going?

Dragon-Snake: My son is sick, and I'm looking for a doctor.

Doctor: How old is your son?

Dragon-Snake: He's a year old.

Doctor: Sorry, but I'm not feeling well.

The dragon-snake leaves the house and comes back later. The song is repeated as the son becomes two, then three years old, all the way up to 10.

Doctor: Dragon-Snake, where are you going?

Dragon-Snake: My son is sick, and I am looking for a doctor.

Doctor: How old is your son?

Dragon-Snake: He's 10 years old.

Doctor: Well, well! The doctor is here. But first, give me the head.

Dragon-Snake: Nothing but the bones.

Doctor: Give me the body.

Dragon-Snake: Nothing but the blood.

Doctor: Give me the tail.

Dragon-Snake: No way! See if you can catch it.

Angry, the doctor chases the dragon-snake and tries to catch the last person in line, who stands in for the tail. During the chase, the dragon-snake spreads out its arms to block the doctor from snatching the tail. If the dragon-snake can form a circle before the doctor touches the tail, the dragon-snake wins. But if the doctor grabs the tail, then he or she wins. The dragon-snake team puts both hands out with their palms up and the doctor slaps them one by one. The tail then becomes the doctor, and the game begins again!

A Traditional Board Game

Ô Ăn Quan is a board game many Vietnamese adults remember playing as kids. You can use a game board or just draw a simple outline with chalk. The idea is to capture the other player's pieces. Fruit seeds, stones, plastic pieces: anything can be used. The player with the most pieces in the end wins!

Are You Superstitious?

The Vietnamese have a long list of dos and don'ts. There are things that bring good luck and drive away bad luck. The three cousins know all about these superstitions. Before a big test at school, they know there are certain foods to avoid if they want to get a good grade.

> When I was little, I used to wear a tiger's claw for protection so I wouldn't cry at night or have bad dreams.

> Grandma always warns us not to break the fish sauce bottle because it brings bad luck.

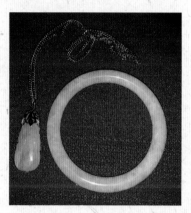

Jade has the ability to heal. Wearing a jade bracelet or charm brings luck, good and prosperity. Women wear frog rings for good fortune and protection.

> My mom reminds me not to praise a baby, or if I do, to add the words trộm viá, which mean "stolen soul." My father's parents are from the North. It's a custom there.

The whale eyes on a boat are intended to help it find its way back to land.

Do or Don't?

- Don't use knives and scissors at New Year, as they might cut off your good fortune.
- Pregnant women are not supposed to go to weddings or funerals. They're seen as bad luck.
- Don't get your hair cut before an exam. It might cause memory loss.
- Stick to odd numbers. Visitors will light one, three or five incense sticks at funeral services.
- Don't shake your legs when you're sitting. Otherwise your luck and your money will fall out.

Knives are to be avoided at New Year.

Let's Make A Beaded Dragonfly!

We've met some of the real and imaginary animals found in Việt Nam and that are of special importance to its people. One tiny creature is a common sight flitting among water lilies or darting along the Mekong shore: the dragonfly. Follow these easy steps to make one of your own!

YOU WILL NEED
1 pipe cleaner
22 assorted color beads (10–12 mm)
Wings template (printed out in landscape mode)
Glue (optional)

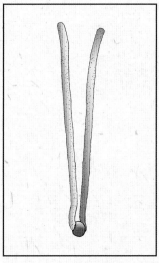

1. Insert one bead into the pipe cleaner and fold in half.

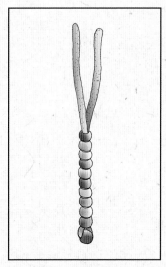

2. Bring the two ends together and insert 10 beads onto it.

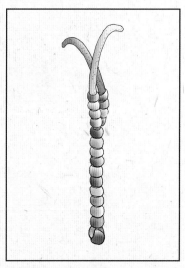

3. Separate the pipe cleaner in two and insert 4 beads onto each side. Twist it together to make the body. Add one bead over the two pipe cleaner ends and twist it again.

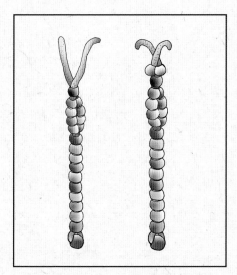

4. Add one bead (of the same color) on each side to make the eyes and twist it. Curl the two ends to make the antennas.

5. Cut out and insert the paper wings into the body.

And your dragonfly is ready to fly!

HINT: You may need to bend the wings slightly to insert them. You may need to glue the wings to the body.

The Areca Nut and the Betel Leaves

Two brothers, Tân and Lang, lived in a small village. Both their parents died when they were young. While Tân was older by a year, both boys looked almost identical. The brothers did everything together—from studying to playing. Everyone in the village had a hard time telling them apart. Even their teacher often mistook Tân for Lang.

Since Tân and Lang were good students and loved to learn, the teacher let them stay at his house. He had a daughter who was in the same class as Tân and Lang. The three were good friends and always studied together. Years passed and the boys grew up to be successful young men. The teacher was impressed with how the two turned out. His daughter also admired her friends for their talent, kindness and intelligence.

Soon it was time for the teacher to look for a husband for his daughter. He wanted to choose one of his very best students, Tân or Lang. In Việt Nam, it was a custom to have the oldest child marry first. "How do I know which one is the oldest brother," the teacher thought. Then a brilliant idea came to him. The next day, he asked his daughter to serve a special meal to both bothers, telling her to leave one bowl and a pair of chopsticks on the table.

Hiding behind the bamboo curtain, the teacher noticed that Lang respectfully offered the bowl and the pair of chopsticks to Tân. It is traditional in Việt Nam to pay respect to the oldest person at the table by passing the food to him or her first. The teacher confidently knew that Tân was the oldest brother. "Since Tân is older, he should be married first," the teacher said. The next day, he asked Tân to marry his daughter.

A celebration was held on the wedding day. Since Lang and Tân were so close, Tân invited Lang to live with him and his new wife in their humble home. Each day the three would go into the rice fields and work from sunrise to sunset. At night they would take walks in the garden together and sit under the moonlight telling stories. Over time, though the three of them were very close, Lang became lonelier and lonelier. But he kept these feelings to himself.

One day while working hard in the field, Tân's wife went home first to prepare dinner. As she started cooking the rice and frying the fish in the little kitchen, she heard someone coming through the front door. It was dark and she thought it was her husband Tân coming home. So she ran out and gave him a hug. She then went back to cooking without realizing that it was actually Lang. Lang was too stunned to say anything and quickly left the house. Ashamed and heartbroken, he decided to go away and leave the happy couple alone. For days he wandered in the forest. The sun beat down on him during the day and the rain pelted his skin in the evenings. After days of walking without any food and water, he came upon a stream. He sat down to rest and the next morning he was nowhere to be seen. All that was left was a giant white rock.

Back at home, Tân and his wife were worried about Lang. They visited every home in the village to see if anyone knew where he was. But no one had seen him. After several days, Tân decided to go and look for his brother. For days he wandered in the forest looking for signs of Lang. Finally Tân reached the stream with the giant white rock. Very tired, Tân rested on the

rock and drank from the stream. The next morning, there was no trace of Tân either. In his place stood a tall tree bearing nuts.

Tân's wife began to worry when neither Tân or Lang returned. She decided to search for them and made the same journey into the forest. She became more and more tired with each step and blisters covered her feet. After days of walking, she arrived at the stream where Tân and Lang had rested. She leaned against the white rock and sought shade under the tall tree. The next morning, there was no sign of her. In her place was a vine that wrapped around the tree with bright green leaves.

When the three did not return, the villagers sent out a search party. When they stopped at the stream, they realized that Lang, Tân and the devoted wife had turned into the stone, tree and vine. The white limestone represented the pure and gentle Lang. The sturdy tree with betel nuts stood for the caring and strong Tân, always watching over his younger brother. The vine wrapped around the tree symbolized Tân's wife, who provided support and strength for her husband.

One day, King Hùng passed by the village and heard the tragic love story. He picked some of the green leaves and chewed them with a slice of areca nut and limestone. He noticed that the mixture produced a dark red juice like the color of blood. It tasted delicious.

To honor the devotion and love that existed between the three, during wedding ceremonies in Việt Nam, the groom's family offers traditional gifts to the bride's family, including a tray of areca nuts, betel leaves and a limestone paste called Mâm Trầu Cau.

Vietnamese Customs and Etiquette

Hải Dương is learning the spoken and unspoken rules that are part of everyday life in Việt Nam. She always shows respect to her host family, but what are some of the other things she's learned?

Street Eats

Arranged on the sidewalk or along the streets, locals and tourists sit in brightly colored plastic chairs. There they enjoy tasty snacks or whole meals they buy at the street vendors' food stalls. Like a mobile mini restaurant, vendors carry their pots and pans, bowls and chopsticks, stove and the most important part—the food!—in their đòn gánh: a long bamboo pole with two baskets hanging from the ends.

Time for a Squat

Vietnamese people of all ages are squatting experts. They don't sit on the ground, but instead they prefer to squat, because they have their own comfortable and imaginary chair wherever they go.

How to Squat the Vietnamese Way

1 While standing up, put both feet flat on the ground, spread slightly apart.
2 Lower the body with your bottom touching the ankles and thighs touching your chest.
3 Spread your knees slightly apart with your torso leaning a little bit forward.

A Few Rules to Follow

• Don't put your hands in your pocket or cross your arms or legs when speaking to someone.
• Pointing or gesturing with chopsticks, or licking them, is considered bad manners.
• Gifts are meant to be opened in private, unless you're asked to open it right away in front of everyone.

Crossing the Street

The nation's cities and towns are known for their traffic jams. Motorbikes, cars and bikes flow down the often clogged streets. Sometimes it looks like a mass of vehicles spreading as far as the eye can see. For tourists especially, crossing the street can be an adventure. Look both ways, then look both ways again! Drivers flow and swerve around the people crossing to the other side.

Hands-On Eating

When eating with chopsticks, it's O.K. to pick up the bowl and hold it close to your mouth. When passing dishes, always use both hands. That's considered polite.

Shoes Off

Shoes and sandals are removed not only outside temples and holy sites but also before entering private homes.

Body Language

- Bowing: A sign of great respect.
- Avoiding eye contact: Shows respect to elders, a stranger or a boss.
- Crossing your middle and index fingers: This is considered a rude gesture.
- Winking: Another sign of bad manners that should be avoided.
- Pointing with the middle finger: It's used instead of the index finger when gesturing toward something.
- The V sign: A way to say "hello" since the Vietnamese word for the number two is "hai," which sounds like the greeting "Hi" in English.

The Palm Leaf Hat & Long Dress

A nón lá, or leaf hat, is made of palm leaves and held on the head by a silk ribbon. It's a practical hat, easy to make and used by the farmers, fishermen and Vietnamese women of all ages in fields, in markets and on city streets. Versions of the hat, with their own unique features, can be found across Việt Nam. The nón bài thơ, or poem hat, is worn in Huế. A nón gò găng can be seen in Bình Định Province, while the nón quai thao graces the heads of people in the North.

Traditional Hats Have Many Uses

As protection from the sun and rain

As a basket for carrying fruits or vegetables

As a container for water

As a fan on hot days

As a way of shielding the face

As a screen for privacy

As a prop for a traditional dance

Custom made to create a perfect fit

The áo dài has split sides and is worn with pants underneath.

Huế women love to wear purple Áo dài.

The Long Dress

Áo dài means "long dress." It's a traditional garment worn throughout the nation. The men's version is shorter and mostly worn on special occasions. Every áo dài is custom made to create a perfect fit. The dress splits into a front and back panel from the waist down and is worn over black or white pants.

Women in traditional hats repair fishing nets.

A short version of Áo dài known as Áo bà ba.

The Legend of Trống Cơm

Despite studying very hard, a poor scholar failed his final exams. He ended up living on the streets and begging for food. Each day, he passed by a big house where a young woman waited to give him some rice. Deeply touched by her kindness and generosity, he came to the house one last time to thank her before leaving town.

A man adds calligraphy as the finishing touches on the red drum he's made.

To his surprise, he learned that she was a servant there. It was the house's owner who told her to give him the rice. He asked to see this generous woman to thank her in person. She had a peaceful face and a beaming smile. The scholar knelt before her, bowed and offered his thanks. Softly the woman said, "Please stand up. There's nothing to thank me for. I understand your bad luck. As you're going far away, here's some money. Please keep this hairpin also as a lucky charm. One day I hope you'll come back to tell us of your many achievements."

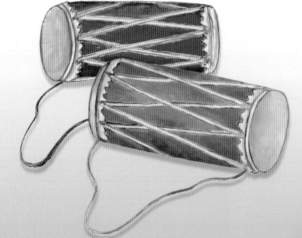

As the years passed, he became a famous and successful musician. He always kept the lucky hairpin with him. One day, he decided to return and visit the owner of the house. But he was too late—she had recently died.

To honor her, he decided to make a red wooden drum. He filled both ends with warm steamed rice in the middle of drum skin so the

instrument could be tuned. The drum was his way of paying tribute to the generous woman. He hung the drum over his neck with a white cloth as a symbol of mourning. Let's learn a song about the Trống Cơm and a dance that goes with it. Let's learn both!

A family of rice drum dancers

The Rice Drum

Vietnamese Folk Song
Arranged by Lê Văn Khoa
English translation by Phước Trần

47

The Rice Drum Dance

Among the traditional dances with fans, conical hats and lanterns, the trống cơm dance is one of the most popular dances in Vietnam. Performers in their colorful áo tứ thân (traditional northern four-part dress) clap both ends of the wooden drums that hang from their necks. The drum hangs on its side near the waist. The tube-shaped body of the drum is made of wood. A string is looped through holes at each end. They create a zigzag pattern.

Follow Along to the Lyrics

Step 1 Beat the drum with both hands when the music starts.
"My love with a rice drum..."

Step 2 Right hand up and down.
"Beautifully..."

Step 3 Left hand up and down.
"Beats a drum..."

Step 4 Both hands beat the drum four times.
"A happy flock of swamp hens..."

Step 5 Rolling both arms upward, move up four steps and dip.
"A happy flock of swamp hens..."

Step 6 Rolling both arms backward, move back four steps and dip.
"Swimming in the river..."

Step 7 Swimming strokes three times.
"Where would it be?..."

Step 8 Right hand on the forehead and move head left to right.
"I miss my love..."

Step 9 Both hands crossed on the chest.
"Both eyes are flickering..."

Step 10 Fingers open and closed ten times.
"A group of spiders spinning..."

Step 11 Rolling upward both arms and move up four steps and dip.
"Where would it be?"

Step 12 Extend both hands to the right and spinning around.
"I miss my love..."

Step 13 Both hands crossed on the chest.
"Where is my love?"

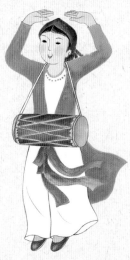

Step 14 Move left to right two times and pose with right hand up and left hand down.

Now it's time to repeat the song!

It's Time to Celebrate!

We've already celebrated Tết, Vietnamese New Year. That's the most important event in Việt Nam. But what are some of the other colorful festivals, holidays and celebrations spread throughout the year? From the Cold Food Festival to the Feast of the Wandering Souls, there are many reasons to get together and celebrate in Việt Nam.

The Mid-Autumn Festival

Tết Trung Thu always falls on the fifteenth day of the eighth month. It's a time for family reunions, eating moon cakes and outdoor activities such as the lantern parade and the lion dance. It's also a night for couples to sit on hilltops watching for the brightest moon of the year. Children can be seen parading on the streets, singing and carrying colorful lanterns.

The Trần Temple Festival

One of the largest annual spring festivals, it's celebrated on the fifteenth day of the first month. The event takes place in Nam Định. Incense is burned at the tombs of the kings, then the gates of the temples and shrines are opened. A parade filled with colorful dancers honors the Trần kings. Games and contests are also part of the fun, including a famous rice-cooking challenge.

Moon Cakes

People set up altars in family courtyards under the moon with moon cakes and plates of round fruits—pomegranates, peaches, persimmons and grapes. Special dishes are served, including nine-jointed lotus roots (symbols of peace) and watermelons cut in the shape of lotus petals (symbols of reunion). Tea is also sipped from small cups under the bright light of the moon.

Other Lunar Calendar Festivals

- **Double Feast Festival**—The fifth day of the fifth month Lễ Đoan Ngọ
- **Double Seven Festival**—The seventh day of the seventh month Lễ Thất Tịch/Lễ Ngưu Lang Chức Nữ
- **Feast of the Wandering Souls**—The fifteenth day of the seventh month Lễ Vu Lan
- **Moon Festival**—The fifteenth of the eighth month Tết Trung Thu
- **The Kitchen God Festival**—The twenty-third day of the twelfth month Lễ Ông Táo Về Trời

Lễ Phật Đản is an important holiday for Buddhists. It falls on the eighth day of the fourth month in the lunar calendar.

The Hùng Kings' Festival

This special day honors the memory of Việt Nam's early kings. A hundred lanterns are released into the sky on the eve of the festival, which includes a flower ceremony and a long procession to the temple on top of the mountain. Participants are treated to performances of classical songs and operas along the way.

Buddha's Birthday

Lanterns float on a nighttime river to celebrate Buddha's birthday. The delicate "birthday candles" are made from lotus-flower-shaped cups of papers. A lit candle is then balanced in the center. Ceremonies are held across Việt Nam. Monastaries offer programs, and Buddhists gather on Yên Tử Mountain. Statues of a newborn Buddha are also bathed in basins.

The Hội An Lantern Festival

On the fourteenth day of each month, the central Vietnamese city of Hội An turns off its lights. Why? To show off the light of the full moon and the candlelit lanterns floating down the Thu Bồn River. The river's banks fill up with locals and tourists seeking a good spot to view the glowing water. February's is the largest and most dazzling festival. The first full moon of the lunar new year marks the biggest celebration of all.

Let's Make Moon Cakes!

You've read about the sights and sounds of the Mid-Autumn Festival. Now it's time to taste the sweet treats made especially for this time of year. Ask an adult to help you bake these fall favorites that work as desserts or an after-school snack.

Moon Cakes

You don't need a moon cake mold to try these festival favorites at home. Cupcake pans or ramekins can be used or just place balls of batter wrapped around the filling on a baking sheet. You'll smell the cakes before you taste them, the odor wafting through your kitchen!

8 SERVINGS

½ cup (100 g) all-purpose flour
½ cup (100 g) cake flour
⅓ cup (120 g) honey
2 tablespoons sunflower or vegetable oil
1 tablespoon peanut or almond butter
1 egg yolk
¼ teaspoon baking soda
One 7.4-oz (210-g) can red bean or 2 cups (450 g) almond paste
1 large egg
1 tablespoon water or milk

1. Preheat your oven to 350 F (175 C). Mix all ingredients together, except for the paste (the first seven ingredients listed). Use a spatula to stir and mix well, then hand-knead for 5 minutes so the dough becomes soft and shiny. Wrap it in plastic and refrigerate for 30 minutes.
2. Lightly oil the palms of your hands. Portion the almond paste or red bean paste into 8 balls and the dough into 8 balls. Flatten each ball into a 4-inch (10-cm) circle and wrap it around the red bean or almond paste. Combine the egg and water or milk to prepare the egg wash.
3. Bake the mooncakes for 5 minutes on the oven's middle rack. Take them out and brush the surface with egg wash and bake them again for another 10 minutes or until golden. Let the mooncakes cool completely and store them in the dry place for one or two days before serving.

NOTE: Moon cake molds in different sizes and designs can be purchased at an Asian market or online.

THE CARP THAT BECAME A DRAGON

Let's Make a Jumping Fish!

There is a popular tale about Cá Hóa Rồng, a carp who turns into a dragon. Parents use the story to teach their kids about patience and hard work. For the fish template, here's the link you'll need: www.tuttlepublishing.com/all-about-vietnam.

YOU WILL NEED:
Colored paper for the fish template
Scissors
Markers
Yarn
Glue stick

1 Fold and unfold the square paper in half to form a crease.

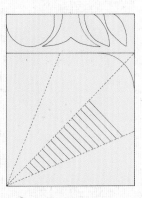

2 Fold both sides to the center to form a point at the bottom.

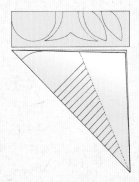

3 Unfold the paper and cut alongside the lined paper tip to the crease of the paper.

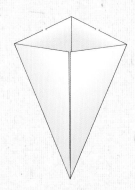

4 Round the point off to make the fish mouth.

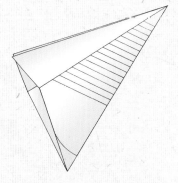

5 Open it up again to the original square, then take one of the quarter-folds and put some glue on it.

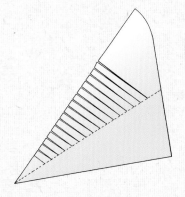

6 Glue the two quarter-triangles together.

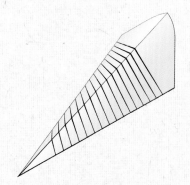

7 Cut fins, mouth and a tail for the fish.

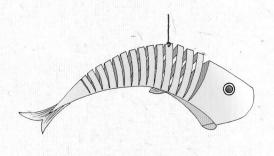

8 Draw the two eyes. Tie the yarn to the fish body.

Have You Tried These Fruits?

We spent the day exploring the orchards of the Mekong Delta. So many delicious and unique fruits grow there! We ate our fill. From there, we caught sight of the beautiful flame tree and watched women gather water lilies with their bright blossoms and long stems.

Cashew Apple Điều

Once picked, these pear-shaped apples last only a few days. They have a sweet and tangy taste. They can be eaten fresh or cut into pieces and dipped in salt and chili powder.

Star Apple Vú Sữa

With its shiny violet or green skin, the star apple is pressed and rolled to release its milky juice. Then a hole is made at the bottom, and the juice is sucked out. It can also be cut in half and scooped out with a spoon.

Mangosteen Măng Cụt

Also called the Queen of the Fruits, this sweet treat has a deep purple rind. Bình An used to learn numbers by counting how many petal patterns are at the bottom of the fruit. This equals the number of sections inside.

Sweetsop or Custard Apple Mảng Cầu Ta

A green, cone-shaped fruit with a scaly rind, the sweet, creamy white pulp has a lot of shiny black seeds, which can't be eaten.

Jackfruit Mít

The largest fruit in the world, it has a rubbery, spiky rind. The sweet, yellow pulp can be eaten fresh or used to make a variety of dishes. The seeds are boiled or roasted for a snack. The golden wood of the jackfruit tree is used for making statues, furniture and barrels.

Longan Long Nhãn

A relative of the lychee, its name means "dragon's eyes." Its pulp, covered in a brownish peel, has a sweet smell. The hard and shiny black seeds can't be eaten. Children use them to make beautiful rings. Dried pieces of longan are also cooked in water and rock sugar to make a delicious dessert.

Durian Sầu Riêng

Known as the King of Fruits, they can weigh up to 7 pounds (3.2 kg). With thick and thorny rinds, this fruit's claim to fame is its strong, unpleasant odor. For those who can stand the smell, the amazing taste is worth it. Durian trees bear fruit only once a year.

The Flame Tree

A popular and poetic symbol of Việt Nam is the flame tree. Called phượng vĩ or "phoenix's tale, see" (see page 30), it's a common sight in city parks and along roadsides. It's known for its fern-like leaves and red-orange flowers that appear from May through July.

Water Lilies

In fall, when the Mekong Delta floods, water lilies pop up by the thousands. From early September to mid-November, they're gathered and sent to market. The flowers are used for decoration or food. The stalks can be eaten, and the entire plant can be made into tea.

Fold Your Own Paper Lotus

The lotus can be found throughout Việt Nam floating in city park or temple ponds and blooming along the Mekong Delta. Every part of the lotus is used either as medicine or food. Lotus seeds can be eaten raw, roasted or boiled. The dried stamens—the thin tube-like part inside the petals—are made into an herbal tea that helps you fall asleep.

1 You'll need 6 rectangles of the same color paper for the petals and 3 rectangles of green paper for the leaves. You can use any size rectangle (1½ x 3 inches or 3.8 x 7.6 centimeters works well), but they all need to the same size. You'll also need a rubber band and a pipe cleaner.

2 To make the petals, take one sheet of the non-green paper and fold it in half to make a center crease. The open up the folded piece.

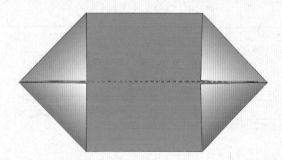

3 Fold the four corners to the center crease.

4 Fold the two long sides to the center crease.

5 Now fold the paper in half lengthwise so that the folded parts can be seen on the outside.

6 Repeat Steps to 2 to 5 for each of the remaining 5 petals.

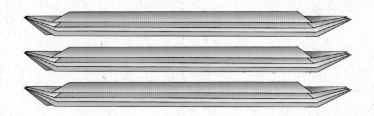

7 To make the leaves, use the green paper and repeat Steps 2 to 4.

8 Then, to finish the leaf, fold the paper lengthwise, with the smooth side facing out. Repeat the steps for each leaf.

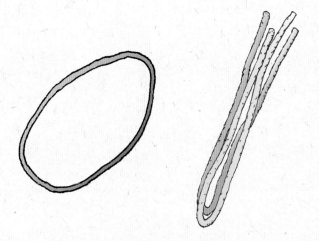

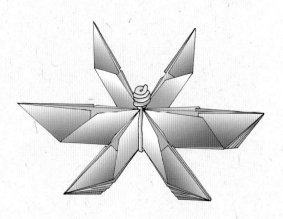

9 To assemble the flower, you will make three separate "packets." Take one petal and place it inside another petal. Then take a leaf and lay it inside the two petals. Repeat this step for the remaining leaves and petals so you have three packets total.

10 Put the three packets side to side (with the long sides touching each other) with the open side up. Put a rubber band around the middle tightly. Then twist a pipe cleaner, preferably yellow, around to form the stamen.
11 Then turn the flower upside down and gently lift the leaves and petals halfway up.
12 You can shape the petals as necessary to give your creation the perfect lotus shape.

My Favorite Places in Việt Nam

Hải Dương's trip is coming to an end, and she wants to show family and friends back home some of the amazing places she's been. So many new memories, it's hard to choose. Here are just some of the highlights of Hải Dương's once-in-a-lifetime trip.

Dear Auntie Lộc,

The Sapa Hills look like green stairways. The rice fields here follow the twisty, turning curves of the land. We hiked along the rice terraces, visited some local villages and went swimming in the Fairy Cave.

Dear Ý Vy,

Why do some of the churches and cathedrals in Sài Gòn look like they could belong in France? The French once ruled Việt Nam. So traces of the French can still be seen in the way some of the city's churches are styled and designed.

Dear Teacher Nam,

The markets of Hà Nội are filled with a rainbow of colors. The incense sellers need to dry their sticks in the sun before sending them to their stalls.

Dear Joshua,

Look where I was today: SƠN ĐOÒNG CAVE, the largest cave in the world! Light shines down through sinkholes overhead, allowing a forest to grow inside the cave. An entire New York City block could fit inside this cavern, the skyscrapers included!

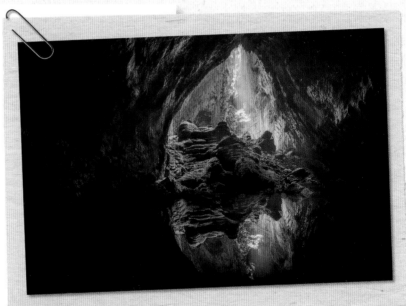

Dear Uncle Trung,

Sun World is an amusement park in the BÁ NÁ HILLS. We took a cable car to get there and crossed the Golden Bridge. It's held up by two huge hands. They look like a stone giant is reaching out of the mountain.

Goodbye and Come Back Again!

"It's hard to say goodbye to Việt Nam and my newfound family and friends," Hải Dương says to her cousins. "But I can't wait to come back!" When Vietnamese people greet or say goodbye to one another, they use the word Chào to start with. How does Hải Dương say goodbye and thank you to her relatives and friends?

To her grandparents:

Dạ thưa ông bà ngoại, mấy bác, mấy cậu, mấy dì con đi về!

Goodbye to my maternal grandparents, great uncles and aunts, I'm going home!

To her cousins Bình An and Nguyệt Thu:

Dạ cám ơn anh chị! Em đi về!
Thank you, I'm going home!

To her younger cousins:

Chào em, chị về!
Goodbye, I'm going home!

To her new friends:

Chào các bạn tôi về!
Goodbye, I'm going home!

Here are some other ways of saying goodbye in different settings and situations:

Goodbye to parents when leaving home for school

Dạ thưa ba má con đi học, literally means I am going to school

Goodbye to a teacher when going home:

To a female teacher: Dạ thưa cô em về!
To a male teacher: Dạ thưa thầy em về!

Goodbye to a boss or older person:

Dạ xin chào! or Dạ xin phép!

Younger people love to say Bai, which means "Bye" in English

Bai, gặp lại sau!
Bye, see you later!

Xin chào Việt Nam!
Goodbye, Vietnam!

Greetings or Goodbyes

For older woman	Chào bà	Chow bah
For older man	Chào ông	Chow ong
For younger woman	Chào cô	Chow ko
For younger man	Chào cậu	Chow kow!
For children	Chào em	Chow [e]m
For man about your age or older	Chào anh	Chow anh
For woman about your age or older	Chào chị	Chow chee

The Children of Việt Nam

Hải Dương has met so many new friends on her travels, it's hard to remember them all. Kids on the move, families on the go. So much to explore and so many new people to meet. She can't wait to come back and continue her Vietnamese adventures!

Headed to a family Christmas celebration in Ha Noi.

A chain of kids winds along the rice terraces of Yên Bái.

Hmong kids at a market in Ha Giang Province.

Cousins enjoy barbecue in Làng Nướng.

Time for a squat in Raglai.

Brothers explore the Bà Nà Hills for the first time.

MY VIỆT NAM FACT FILE
Did You Know?

Official name:
Socialist Republic of Việt Nam
Capital: Hà Nội

Area: 127,123 square miles
(329,247 square kilometers)

Major National Holiday:
November 20 (Teacher's Day)

National Flower: Lotus

Shaped Like the Letter "S"

● The country lies on the eastern edge of the area known as Indochina.
● Việt Nam's neighbors: China to the north, Laos and Cambodia to the west
● Its eastern border is a 1,000-mile coastline along the South China Sea.
● The mountains of the Annam Cordillera run along most of the western border.

FAST FACTS

There are about 45 million motorbikes in Việt Nam.

Việt Nam is the world's largest producer of cashews.

Books and Websites to Explore

Further Reading

Bao Phi. *A Different Pond*, 2017.

Minh Le. *Lift*, 2020.

Tram Le and Tri C Tran. *Vietnamese Stories for Language Learners*, 2017.

Tran Thi Minh Phuoc and illustrators Nguyen Thi Hop and Nguyen Dong: *My First Book of Vietnamese Words: An ABC Rhyming Book of Language and Culture*, 2017.

Tran Thi Minh Phuoc and illustrators Nguyen Thi Hop and Nguyen Dong: *Vietnamese Children's Favorite Stories*, 2015.

Websites

National Geographic for Kids
kids.nationalgeographic.com/ geography/countries/article/vietnam

Vietnamese Heritage Museum: People around the world can retrieve documents, stories, testimonies of the history of Vietnamese refugees who fled Việt Nam after the Vietnam War.
www.vietnameseheritagemuseum.org

www.teachingbooks.net/ pronunciations.cgi
A collection of brief recordings of authors and illustrators saying their names.

www.teachingbooks.net/pronounce. cgi?pid=2317
Pronunciation of the author's name.

Index

Dedications

This book is dedicated to my dear family, my awesome friends, and my curious readers who love to learn about Việt Nam and its people.   —**Trần Thị Minh Phước**

We dedicate this book, which contains our vision and reminiscences of Việt Nam, to our daughter, Danchi.
—**Nguyễn Thị Hợp & Nguyễn Đồng**

"Books to Span the East and West"

Tuttle Publishing was founded in 1832 in the small New England town of Rutland, Vermont [USA]. Our core values remain as strong today as they were then—to publish best-in-class books which bring people together one page at a time. In 1948, w established a publishing office in Japan—and Tuttle is now a leader in publishing English-language books about the arts, languages and cultures of Asia. The world has become a much smaller place today and Asia's economic and cultural influence has grown. Yet the need for meaningful dialogue and information about this diverse region has never been greater. Over the past seven decades, Tuttle has published thousands of books on subjects ranging from martial arts and paper crafts to language learning and literature—and our talented authors, illustrators, designers and photographers have won many prestigious awards. We welcome you to explore the wealth of information available on Asia at **www.tuttlepublishing.com**.

Photo Credits

p7 Châu Thụy; p17 Trần Minh Nhật & Xuân Lộc; p19 Hoàng Sơn Hồng; p21 Danchi Nguyen; p24, 25, 36 Trần Phương Mai & Trần Giang; p25 Trần Minh Chánh & Trịnh Kim Các; p33, p45 Hồ Thị Như Mai; p36, 61 Trần Thị Minh Lộc & Nguyễn Trần HảiDương; p36, 43, 62 Joseph Kerr; p44, 51 Nguyễn Quốc Thịnh; p45 Hạnh Trần; p46 Nguyễn Trần Thuỳ Dương; p47 Lê Văn Khoa; p58 Tân Phạm; p61 Trần Minh Tú

iStock.com—p7: below left 46838384©cristaltran

Shutterstock.com—p5: below left 1127931986©TOM...foto; below right 1103353646© pradeep_kmpk14 p7: top right 64310887©kowit sitthi; below right 1871767702©Huy Thoai p14: top 1218764575©Nguyen Quang Ngoc Tonkin; below left 600215705©Mikhail Gnatkovskiy; below right 26832019©inavanhateren p15: top right 256004092©Vietnam Stock Images; below right 1549845485©Vietnam Stock Images p16: top 586600610©TBone Lee; below left 681882106©DMHai; below right 1303493764©Tang Trung Kien p17: top right 1711063348© Marie Shark; middle right 1391562959©vivanvu; bottom left 1496069360©sal73it p18: top 199933784©Frank Fischbach p19: top right 1190849821©Vietnam Stock Images; middle right 1599744724©Jangqq p20: top 1578296776©ngoc tran p21: top right 1171701622©Khanthachai C p24: bottom right 1569731155©Ho Su A Bi p25: top right 1344929519©Wachiwit bottom left 1461473810©Nguyen Quang Ngoc Tonkin; below right 1102013459©Yavuz Sariyildiz p26: left to right 1160816530©Joshua Resnick; 501336490©AS Food studio; 1213499995©fotobycam; middle left 1659721459©Marie Sonmez Photography; middle right 698789653©Vietnam Stock; bottom 1866768322©hecke61 p27: below left 616309328©Yarygin; below right 1116581642© David Bokuchava p28: 208334329©Brent Hofacker p29: 1901634559©Chzu p31: top left 190172681©WathanyuSowong; top right 146022089©Dobino; below left 198573980©TigerStocks; below right 610844717©Asia Images p32: below 1924411085©KernelNguyen p33: top left 1549268666©TuanAnhNgo p42: top left 417920380©JunPhoto; top right 417920380©JunPhoto; below left 1512809225©evgenii mitroshin; below right 1526342717©TommoT; bottom 1657620166©gpointstudio p43: middle left 113719546©Kristyn Kowalewski; middle right 1156756684©Matt Hahnewald; bottom 293161223©Stephane Bidouze p45: top 1771250912© Tran Qui Thinh; bottom 1178121070©Vadim Petrakov p46: top 1520328380©JACKY HO p50: top 1169172481©vivanvu; middle 1801419865©Lusin_da_ra; bottom 1169172481© Phuong-Thao p51: middle left 1134207371©Huy Thoai; middle right 1719214567©Berry Phan; bottom 1477602647©JomNicha p52: 310420856@Cao Phuong p54: bottom left 247676617@ Tukaram.Karve; bottom right 597185463@ pukao p55: top left 1165410619©Wealthylady; top right 1145070053©Torjrtrx; below left 283773239©Suzana Tran; below right 1109113379© Vietnam Stock Images p58: top 487942870©JunPhoto p59: top 1698525367© saravutpics; middle 1487628662©Hoang Trung; bottom & content page 1343287217©Hien Phung Thu p61: top left 765307795©NguyenQuocThang; top right 329358482©TZIDO SUN; middle left 228302659© Van Thanh Chuong p62: top right 1884334984©olenadesign; below right 1568872894©Sakcared

Published by Tuttle Publishing, an imprint of Periplus Editions (HK) Ltd.

www.tuttlepublishing.com

Copyright ©2022 Trần Thị Minh Phước
Illustrations Copyright ©2022 Nguyen Thi Hop & Nguyen Dong

Copyright ©2022 Periplus Editions (HK) Ltd.

Library of Congress Cataloging-in-Publication Data in Process

This edition ISBN 978-0-8048-4693-6

Distributed by

North America, Latin America & Europe
Tuttle Publishing
364 Innovation Drive
North Clarendon, VT 05759-9436 U.S.A.
Tel: (802) 773-8930
Fax: (802) 773-6993
info@tuttlepublishing.com
www.tuttlepublishing.com

Asia Pacific
Berkeley Books Pte. Ltd.
3 Kallang Sector, #04-01
Singapore 349278
Tel: (65) 6741-2178
Fax: (65) 6741-2179
inquiries@periplus.com.sg
www.tuttlepublishing.com

First edition
25 24 23 22
10 9 8 7 6 5 4 3 2

Printed in China
2206EP

TUTTLE PUBLISHING® is a registered trademark of Tuttle Publishing, a division of Periplus Editions (HK) Ltd.

How to access the online recordings for this book:

1. Check to be sure you have an internet connection.
2. Type the following URL into your web browser:

https://www.tuttlepublishing.com/all-about-vietnam

For support you can email us at:

info@tuttlepublishing.com